daily delights of love
180 poems to illuminate your heart and soul.

emily monroe

this book is for my love:

_____

for the one who captures my heart:

this is my dedication to you, the one who enchants me daily. through these words, may you feel my love surround you, steadfast and true.

within each page of *daily delight of love,* you'll discover echoes of our laughter and the comfort of our shared silences, the dreams that twine our lives together. these pages are a testament to the cherished moments and the quiet understanding that binds us.

as every new day dawns, know that my heart is with you, resonating in the silent whispers of dawn and the calm of dusk. this book mirrors our journey, the love that enriches our daily existence, and the promise of our continued devotion, encapsulated in the *daily delight of love.* delight that each new day brings, culminating in the everlasting promise of our *daily delight of love.*

introduction

this book is a daily tribute to the love that casts a radiant glow on every facet of our lives. designed for the dreamers, the hopeful, and the eternal optimists, it is a collection of moments filled with the beauty and joy of love in the daily grind. each page reflects the understated yet profound ways love manifests in the ordinary, transforming the mundane into something extraordinary.

as you turn these pages, let them murmur words of affection, acting as a gentle reminder of the love that steadfastly surrounds you, as constant as the sunrise. this is a celebration of the small, daily occurrences that form the foundation of our deepest bonds.

here, you'll find a consistent outpouring of love that echoes with your innermost feelings, lifting your spirit and affirming the notion that in life's regular rhythm, love is the melody that makes every heart beat with more vigor. toast to the love that fills your days, the kind that stays with you, and becomes the sweetest aspect of your everyday life.

to the person i cherish

trust me when i tell you that i have never felt a love like this before.

your presence is my solace, your love, my forevermore.

confusion in my mind
when i wholeheartedly love, yes
with your insights
it fine-tunes my desires, as
i ask once more
for your lips again
your hands again
around my neck again
to linger longer
consume me again
because i love you
and will love you forever

in love, hope is the whispered prayer.
between entwined fingers.
a delicate bloom amidst life's fleeting winters.
it's the promise written in every shared glance,
a dance of hearts that takes a hopeful chance.
love's truest essence it fuels our eternal flight,
in hope,
we find the strength to conquer the darkest night.

in the language of love, gratitude blooms like a
fragrant rose,
thanks whispered in every beat, the sweetest prose.

i'm endlessly grateful for your love, a debt my heart
forever knows.

your love, a gentle whisper in the silence of my soul,
in your embrace,
i find where i truly belong, made whole.
with every beat,
you paint my heart in hues of bliss,
loving you feels like an eternal, tender kiss.

your likeness in love is a beacon,
a guiding light,
in your eyes,
i see stars, painting my darkest night.

trust in love,
a fragile but unbreakable bond we share,
a promise whispered in the wind,
a love beyond compare.

in this vast universe, i choose you, my dear,
you're my compass,
my north star, ever crystal clear.

the best feeling i've ever had,
an echo in my soul,
in your love,
i've found the missing piece to make me whole.

among a million stars,
i'd choose your radiant light,
in your smile, i find courage to face the darkest
night.

the best feeling i've ever known,
like a warm, soft rain,
in your love,
i've found peace amidst life's endless terrain.

in your presence,
 i find shelter,
a sacred,
hallowed place.
trust in love,
 like roots of an ancient,
 steadfast tree,
in your eyes,
 i find the truth that sets my spirit free.

in your love, i've found my haven, my eternal
nightlight,
my sanctuary amidst life's relentless fight.
the best feeling i've ever felt, like a comet's fleeting
blaze,
i've found the sun in a thousand cloudy days.
in your likeness in love, i've found my sanctuary, my
eternal dove, your laughter, my solace, your touch,
my balm, in your love, i've found my eternal calm.

no hurdle too high, no path too rough,
with you, i'll endure, i'll be enough.

in your love's embrace, my spirit will soar,
with you, i'll persist, forevermore.

with just a click, our hearts entwined,
in pixels and codes, a love defined.

through screens, emotions brightly gleam,
a digital dance, a shared dream.
in every message, love's sweet rhyme, our hearts
whisper, transcending time, and space.

in a crowded room, our eyes first met,
a silent spark, a fate we couldn't forget.

amidst the chatter, a connection found,
since that moment, love's seed was sound.

now and forever

your eyes, a universe, vast and deep,
in their depths, promises we'd forever keep.

in that gaze, a story silently spun,
a tale of love, of two becoming one.

until the end of the time

i've never met anyone like you in my life,
in the stormy sea of my existence,
you're my only guiding light.

my life without you?
a turbulent sea,
endlessly vast and tempest torn.

beneath the golden sun, we walked hand in hand,
through fields of wildflowers, in love, we'd stand.
your laughter, a melody, in the soft, sweet breeze,
we painted memories 'neath the swaying trees.
in your eyes, i found a universe so bright,
a beautiful day, dear love, wrapped in pure delight.

under the velvet sky adorned with stars so clear,
we shared whispered secrets, drawing near.
the moon, our silent confidante, softly glowed
above,
in your arms, i found solace, endless love.
the night serenaded us with its gentle tune,
a beautiful night, my love, beneath the mystic moon.

your smile illuminates my life,
casting a radiant glow on even the darkest of days.

your eyes, so full of life, are like vibrant constellations, each sparkle telling a story of boundless energy and endless possibilities.

i'll shield you from hypochondriac fears,
from troubles that on your path may appear,
from injustices and deceit in your days,
from failures drawn in your nature's own ways.

i'll lift you from pains and mood swings' sway,
from obsessions that haunt your day.
i'll defy gravity's hold so tight,
space and light to keep you from age's flight.

and you shall heal from all your ills, i'm sure,
for you're a being special, pure.

and i shall tend to you with love and care,
in a world where you're beyond compare.

i will bring you, above all, silence, and patience,
together, we'll journey the paths leading to essence.

for you're a special being, unique and true,
and i will care for you.

i promise to stand by your side, come what may, my love for you unwavering and true.

in your laughter, i find my joy, in your tears, my comfort. i promise to be your strength in every endeavor.

with each sunrise, my love for you deepens.
i promise to cherish you always,
in light and in shadow.

in every whispered secret and shared dream,
i promise my heart, eternally entwined with yours.
i promise to be your rock in the storm,
your shelter in the rain,
your unwavering support through joy and pain.

i swear to cherish you in every moment, to love you without hesitation or condition, now and for all eternity.
with every beat of my heart, i pledge my devotion to you, promising to be your steadfast companion in this journey of love.

i solemnly vow to stand by your side in times of joy
and sorrow, to be your refuge and strength,
forever and always.
in your eyes, i find my purpose;
in your smile, my endless joy.
i swear to treasure you,
honoring our love with unwavering commitment.

in your presence, i find my home, in your absence, my longing.
i promise my devotion, my love, my everything.

i promise to love you not only for who you are today
but for the person you'll become,
with each passing day.

with this ring, i make a vow, to love you forever,
 here and now.
i promise to be your love, your friend,
your all.

i swear to be the calm in your storms,
the light in your darkness.
 with each sunrise, my love for you deepens,
unyielding and resolute.

with every breath i take, i swear my love to you.
i promise to be your shelter in the rain,
your warmth in the cold,
your love in every moment we share.

in love's sweet dance, we find our song,
a melody that lasts our whole life long.

happiness blooms in love's tender gaze,
with you, my heart forever sways.

unique and rare, our love takes flight,
happiness grows with every day and night.

happiness in your eyes, a sunbeam bright,
our love story, a beacon in the night.

happiness in love, a secret we share,
in your embrace, i find solace beyond compare.

in your eyes, a universe, deep and wise,
a connection unspoken, beneath the skies.
with every smile, a story told,
our hearts entwined, in love we're bold.

your laughter, like music, fills the air,
a symphony of joy, beyond compare.
beneath the moon, our secrets shared,
a love so vast, so greatly dared.

in a world of shadows, you emerged as my guiding
star, the only one who filled my heart with joy, near
and far. you're the beacon in my darkest night, the
sun that lights my day, in your presence, all my fears
and doubts simply fade away.

you've painted my life with hues of happiness and
grace, in your love, i found my sanctuary, my
peaceful place. no one else has ever touched my soul
quite like you do, you're the only one who filled my
heart with light, so true.

no words can truly express the gratitude i feel,
for the depth of your love, so genuine and real.
you've given my life a purpose so divine,
in your presence, i've found my life's genuine sign.

in your presence, i found purpose and meaning,
a guiding light through life's complex screening.
you've infused my days with warmth and cheer,
giving life a sense of purpose that's crystal clear.

you've taught me the beauty of love's endless grace,
in your eyes, i see the reflection of my own face.
you've given my existence depth and hue,
in your love, i've discovered a life entirely new.

no words can truly express the gratitude i feel,
for the depth of your love, so genuine and real.
you've given my life a purpose so divine,
in your presence, i've found my life's genuine sign.

in the canvas of my heart,
you're the brightest hue,
loving you,
i find strength, grace, and love anew.
with each breath, you sculpt dreams into reality,
in your love, i discover endless
possibilities and tranquility.

you entered my life like the morning sun,
dispersing darkness, making shadows run.
with your smile, my world became bright,
in your light, i found endless delight.

in the realm where
perfection seemed a distant dream,
i believed it was but a fleeting, elusive gleam.
then i met your eyes, and eternity i found,
in the depth of our souls, a connection unbound.

under silver skies, i unearthed the truth,
in your eyes, i discovered eternal youth.
perfection resides in those genuine stares,
in that eternity, our destinies entwined, it dares.

you are my sanctuary of light and my island of peace.
together, we can build a better world.

i wish to be the water as you shower,
the sheets where you find rest, hour after hour.
the saturday night burger you devour,
i'd be the taste that makes your heart flower.

i'd become the engine in your car,
ignited by your touch, near or far.
yet, you're never enough, never complete,
in your absence, my heart skips its beat.

i want to be the essence you embrace,
the colors on your lips, a delicate trace.
i long to invade your thoughts like a song,
but the ache deepens when you're gone for long.

i'd transform into the engine of your ride,
suddenly, with my presence, you'd be electrified.

you have this amazing ability to face challenges with a smile, to embrace every opportunity with enthusiasm, and to inspire everyone around you. your determination and kindness never cease to amaze me.

seeing you achieve your goals and overcome
obstacles fills my heart with immense pride.
your passion for life, your creativity, and your
resilience are truly admirable.
remember,
your journey, no matter how challenging, is shaping
you into the incredible person you are becoming.
two lives, one journey together.

i am grateful every day to have you in my life, to witness your growth, and to stand by your side. you are a beacon of light, a force to be reckoned with, and a source of endless inspiration. your strength and compassion make the world a better place.

so, keep shining, keep believing in yourself, and keep being the amazing person you are. i am beyond proud to call you mine.

i can't help but smile, for you are the reason my thoughts dance in the rhythms of love.

throughout the day, my thoughts are consumed by
you, a constant presence in my mind.
your laughter echoes in my thoughts, and your smile
lingers like the warmth of the sun on my skin.

i find myself daydreaming about the moments we've shared and imagining the ones yet to come.
your presence is a sweet distraction, a melody that plays in the background of my day,
 making every moment brighter

in the season of our love,
every moment blooms with the vibrant colors of
passion and tenderness,
painting our hearts with the most beautiful shades of
affection.

every moment we've shared feels like a chapter from a love story, where laughter is the soundtrack, and your smile is the highlight.

in your presence, time slows down, and i savor every glance, every touch, as if they were precious secrets shared between our souls.
with you, every second is a masterpiece, a painting of love that colors my world in
endless shades of happiness.

100% pure love.
mathematics isn't an opinion, and neither is my love
for you.

our love story is crafted from the magic of small moments, each giggle, and shared glance weaving a tale as sweet as candy.

you're the sweetest chocolate life could ever offer,
a delightful treat that melts my heart with every taste.

i'm utterly and endlessly lost in your gaze.
i find myself only in our hearts.

i have few certainties in life, but my unwavering love for you is the strongest of them all.

you are unique.
you no longer resemble anyone since
i fell in love with you

keep your heart pure, despite adversities,
for you are special, and i'll take care of you.
yes, i'll take care of you.

no matter how far i travel in this world,
i won't find anyone more perfect than you.

leaving you? it has never been an option.
you're the best choice of my life.

give me your love, and i'll lift the world

i adore your little quirks as much as your great
qualities. stop being so hard on yourself.
i'll always stand by you, through thick and thin.

i can't stop thinking of you,
just like i can't stop dreaming of you and
i can't stop loving you,
just like i can't stop breathing

in the name of your love,
i've found the courage to dream

love will always be the most beautiful and significant journey of discovery one can embark on.
i've chosen you, my treasure, and i cherish every moment of it.

you are the sole companion i could ever desire,
the only love I could ever yearn for,
should your presence not grace my side.

guess what?
i've always been yours, in every moment,
in every situation

i never thought i'd muster the courage to say it,
but today,
i feel my heart is about to burst,
and i can no longer hide.
i have loved you forever

everyone believes their love is special,
unique,
but ours is more special and unique than others
because there
can't be anyone better than you

you've always inhabited my deepest and most intimate dreams, and now you're a part of my life, filling my heart with joy.

p.s. honestly, i don't know what i did in this life or in past ones to be so fortunate.

i aspire to encounter you a century hence; envision
the world then, a hundred years forward.
among myriad obsidian eyes, 'll recognize yours, ever
more radiant than the day before.

oh, this love – the more it consumes us, the closer
we become.
oh, this love is a beacon that shines brightly.

to you, who found me
in solitude's embrace, fists ready,
back against the wall, in life's fray,
eyes lowered, among the weary,
you gently took me in your arms,
like a leaf carried on a stream,
and together we floated away.

to you, who are the only one in the world,
the sole reason to go all the way
with every breath i take,
when i look at you
after a day filled with words,
without you saying a thing,
everything becomes clear.

to you i write, for i have nothing else.
nothing better to offer than all that i have.

take my time and the magic that, with a single leap,
makes us fly like bubbles.

to you
who took my life and made it so much more,
to you
 who gave meaning to time without measuring it,
to you
 who are my great love and my love so grand.

to you, i saw tears in my hands,
so fragile i could have crushed you,
holding you gently,
and then i witnessed you,
with the strength of an airplane,
taking your life into your hands,
and guiding it to safety

For you,
the most wonderful occurrence in my life,
For you,
who evolves daily yet stays ever constant

the forces of nature converge within you,
you're a rock,
you're a tree,
 you're a hurricane,
you're the horizon that welcomes me as i stray.

your love is the spark that ignites my passion,
turning every day into a love story worth living.
with you, even the ordinary becomes extraordinary.

your breath is my essence
your love is my daily inspiration,
your body is my meditation

our love is not just a word;
it's an action, a daily choice we make to cherish,
respect, and uplift one another

if we gaze upon the same moon, we aren't that far apart after all, connected by the silver threads of our shared dreams

same places, same city, but since your eyes met mine, everything is entirely new—a fresh meaning infused into my life.

don't fret about things that will never be. focus on
what your heart desires, and it will come.
you arrived because my heart had already seen you
before my eyes did.

when i saw you coming,
beautiful just as you are,
it didn't seem possible that
among all these people, you'd notice me.
it felt like flying,
here inside my room,
like the most beautiful dream there is.
i've known you forever,
 and i've loved you for always.

eternal, you embody a moment that defies time,
with neither yesterday nor tomorrow in sight,
everything resides in the present within your heart,
a heart vast and infinite

The moon and stars hold no allure for me,
Nor do the celestial bodies above,
For you embody both moon and stars,
You are my sun, my boundless sky,
To me, you are all,
All I desire to hold,
Infinite...

you're within my soul,
in this vulnerable space,
it all begins with you,
no need for a reason why,
we're flesh and breath.
and there i'll leave you forever,
you're in every part of me,
i feel you descending,
between breath and shiver.

some loves never end,
they take vast turns,
and then they return,
undividable loves,
indissoluble,
inseparable,
for me, you're always the one,
extraordinary,
perfectly ordinary,
close and unattainable,
elusive,
incomprehensible.

but never friends,
for those like us who search,
it's not possible,
to hate each other ever,
for those who love like us,
it would be futile

you, you who are unique,
at least you in the universe,
you're a point that never revolves around me,
a sun that shines for me alone,
like a diamond in the middle of my heart

i come to find you, my heart's desire,
just to see you, set my soul on fire,
your presence, my profound essence,
in your words, i find my presence.
i come to seek you, with reasons to share,
to hear your thoughts, your words so rare,
in you, i see my roots deep and true,
forever bound, me and you.

the best years of our life,
hold me tight,
no night is endless.

you are the solace in my darkest days, the light that illuminates our path. thank you for existing.

i'd like to dedicate to you the most beautiful words
ever written, the most enchanting songs ever sung.
i wish to compose for you the most beautiful
masterpiece ever created, but even that wouldn't be
enough to express my love for you.
i love you.

i adore your little quirks as much as your great
qualities. stop being so hard on yourself.
i'll always stand by you, through thick and thin.

i was thinking of you, and my phone started ringing.
love's coincidences.
the synchronicity of our hearts.

with you, i feel safe; with you, i've found the home
for my heart

falling in love with you was the best decision i ever made, and i'd choose you over and over again

love is having someone who knows your coffee order, your favorite song, and your worst dad joke, and loves you anyway.

being in love means sharing secrets, joking around, and letting you steal the last cookie in the jar.

being crazy in love means dancing like nobody's watching, even when everyone is watching.

i love you even when you can be the weirdest
version of you, and they still find you absolutely
adorable.

supporting each other's dreams, no matter how big or small.

our love is late-night conversations and early
morning cuddles. it's finding beauty in imperfections
and comfort in shared silences

with you, every day is a new page of our story,
written with laughter, trust, and endless affection.
love is not just a feeling;
 it's the way we navigate life together,
hand in hand,
creating our own beautiful world.

love is finding someone who knows all your flaws
and still thinks you're perfect.
it's the silly selfies, the spontaneous adventures, and
the late-night talks about everything and nothing.

your smile brightens my days

i miss you from the depths of my soul.
talk to me.
i need to hear your voice.
i need you, your essence

everything starts with you and from you.
you are the pleasure of my life.
the most beautiful moments of my life have been
with you.
i don't remember my life before you.

i am grateful for every second spent with you,
for they are the building blocks of our forever.

you make me see life from a different perspective,
and everything becomes more beautiful and radiant.
your zest for life overcomes the sadness of my past
and the pain of days gone by.
but now, you're here with me, and everything shines
with a new light.

i love you more than you can imagine.
i feel you more than you could hope.

happiness is made of small yet significant moments.
hearing you hum in the shower, watching the
movement of your hands, and gently tracing the
shape of your lips with a finger – these are the
precious tiles of this enchanting mosaic.
you are the most beautiful miracle in my life.

together,
we are the most beautiful versions of ourselves.

loving you allows me to love myself even more. i see so many parts of me reflected in you. you are my sweet and unyielding mirror.

everything happens for a reason. everything happens at the right moment. i waited for you my whole life. if all my sad moments led me to you, i thank them for the precious gift they gave me.

thank you
for being the calm in the storm of my soul

if you can't change the winds,
adjust the sails.
that's how i sailed to you

the universe brought us together because we are two destinies merging, entwined in a single moment

don't ask too many questions. the answers are
written in our hearts. live every moment. breathe in
our breaths, and everything will come to life

why do i love you?
ask the stars. it's been written since forever.
maktub.

i think of love, thinking of you. you are what i've always hoped for.
i am where i've always wanted to be.

we are truest when we align with our ideal selves,
and we are loved when we embrace the best within
us.

i adore your little quirks as much as your great
qualities. stop being so hard on yourself.
i'll always stand by you, through thick and thin.

i adore your little quirks as much as your great qualities. stop being so hard on yourself. i'll always stand by you, through thick and thin.

i got completely lost in your eyes. i've revisited my past, i'm savoring our present, and i glimpse our future together.

i'll always be by your side. i have faith, and i know that no matter what storm may come, our bow will always be pointing towards you, beside you.

there's no better place than your heart

think i'm crazy for loving you? yes, i am.
it's all a balance on the edge of madness

honestly speaking,
i lost my mind the moment i met your eyes.
there was no way to turn back

legs intertwined,
in the bathtub,
candles casting a soft glow on your face,
a gentle flicker beneath your lips.
hours spent listening to our favorite music,
while everything else faded away,
even the rain.

when i say
i love you,
 i mean i love every part of you,
 from your darkest secrets to your brightest smile.
you are my everything.

every moment spent with you is unique.
you make every moment of our life together special.
it's like living in a dream,
knowing we are awake and happy.

i am yours, and it shows in every cell of my body.

in the moment our eyes first met, my life found its
turning point. there's a before you, and with you,
a whole new chapter begins.

love is a feeling, not a thing.
love is a choice, not a chance.
love is a journey, not a destination.

i love the way you make me feel like i'm home,
wherever we are.

i will be your friend
through thick and thin
i will be your confidant
no matter what the sin

i will be your laughter
when you are feeling blue
i will be your voice of reason
when you are feeling confused

i will be your rock
to lean on when you fall
i will be your light
to guide you through the dark

i will be your everything
to make you feel loved
i will be your best friend
till the very end

when i look into your eyes,
i see the fire that burns inside.
it's a passion that's so strong,
it could melt the coldest stone.

when i touch your skin,
i feel the heat of your desire.
it's a passion that's so pure,
it could light up the darkest night.

when i kiss your lips,
i taste the sweetness of your love.
it's a passion that's so sweet,
it could make me soar above.

when i'm with you,
i feel alive.
your passion is like a drug,
it's addictive and i can't get enough.

i know that our love is real,
because it's fueled by passion.
our passion is a flame that will never die,
it will burn forever in our hearts.

when i first met you,
i didn't know what to expect.
i was just a person,
looking for love.

but when i saw your smile,
i knew that i was found.
you were everything i had ever wanted,
and more.

you made me laugh,
you made me cry,
you made me feel alive.

you showed me what love really is,
and i will never forget you.

the morning light shines through the window,
and i see your face,
so beautiful, so natural,
without a trace of makeup.

your hair is tousled,
your eyes are still sleepy,
and your lips are slightly parted,
as if you're about to speak.

i smile,
and my heart fills with joy,
to see you like this,
in your most natural state.

you are the most beautiful woman i have ever seen,
and i am so grateful to have you in my life.

you are, simply are,
the love of my life.

if i lost you, i'd be losing the love of my life, my best friend, my confidante, my everything.
you make me a better person, and i don't know what i'd do without you.
i love you more than words can say

maybe it's because we're from a distant planet,
but the world from here seems like a secret trapdoor.
everyone wants everything,
only to realize it's nothing.
we won't follow the crowd,
together, these are and will forever remain the best
years of our lives.
hold me tight so that no night feels infinite.

the best years of our lives.

you've taught me to listen,
with empathy and care,
to give and receive love,
without expecting a share.

you've encouraged my dreams,
helped me to forgive,
shown me the beauty,
of the present to live.

thank you, my love,
for all that i've learned.
i'm a better person,
because of you i've turned.

i'll spend the rest of my life loving you the way you
deserve to be loved.
i'll listen to you with empathy and understanding.
i'll support your dreams and passions.
i'll be there for you through thick and thin.
i'll make you laugh, and i'll wipe your tears away.
i'll love you unconditionally,
and i'll never give up on you.

as long as i'm alive,
i'll never let you feel alone.
i'll always be here for you,
to love you and care for you.

you're the most important person in my life,
and i'll never take you for granted.
i absolutely adore you.

falling in love with you was like a force of nature.
 it was something i couldn't control.
the first time i saw you, i knew you were the one.
you're everything i've ever wanted in a partner.
you're beautiful, intelligent, funny, and kind.
i love everything about you.

once weighed down by worries,
my heart now beats light.
in your embrace, i find
a dream without night.

my mind at peace, my soul at ease,
i drift away to sleep.
your love surrounds me like a breeze,
my cares no longer deep.

oh, to fall asleep without a care,
to drift on clouds above.
with you by my side, i know no fear,
my heart filled with your love.

the morning light shines through the window,
and i see your face,
so beautiful, so natural,
without a trace of makeup.

your hair is tousled,
your eyes are still sleepy,
and your lips are slightly parted,
as if you're about to speak.

i smile,
and my heart fills with joy,
to see you like this,
in your most natural state.

you are the most beautiful woman i have ever seen,
and i am so grateful to have you in my life.

you are, simply are,
the love of my life.

when i first met you,
i didn't know what to expect.
i was just a person,
looking for love.

but when i saw your smile,
i knew that i was found.
you were everything i had ever wanted,
and more.

you made me laugh,
you made me cry,
you made me feel alive.

you showed me what love really is,
and i will never forget you.

the morning light shines through the window,
and i see your face,
so beautiful, so natural,
without a trace of makeup.

your hair is tousled,
your eyes are still sleepy,
and your lips are slightly parted,
as if you're about to speak.

i smile,
and my heart fills with joy,
to see you like this,
in your most natural state.

you are the most beautiful woman i have ever seen,
and i am so grateful to have you in my life.

you are, simply are,
the love of my life.

when you first told me you loved me,
i couldn't believe my ears.
i'm not used to this kind of love,
my brain couldn't process it.
but my heart knew - and it felt like i was flying,
a feeling of euphoria i'd never felt before.

your love has changed me,
in so many beautiful ways.
thank you for showing me that true love exists.

come over now,
softly close those beautiful eyes.
watch as sorrows fade away,
the rest, uncertain,
will unfold tomorrow.
i crave to be by your side,
to taste the sweetness of your lips and share with you
in this moment where all things flow,
in a world that's ever-changing,
we remain steadfastly here, together.

and we don't need words
to express what's hidden deep within our hearts
but i'll lift you up
every time you fall
and gather the flowers you might lose along the way
i'll follow your flight
without ever getting in the way
because what i desire
is to be with you
without any constraints
to be with you

unravel your hair, my love
let the sun kiss your skin,
i too caress you with my gaze,
my red rose, my everything.

come closer, my love,
let us ignite this flame,
burn away all your fears,
and dance in the embers of our love

oh, if i were a pigeon,
swooping down from rooftops to his heart.
at least i'd be in that glass,
so when he sips, i'd journey down to his foot.

if, in the afterlife, i could return,
i'd greet you each morning as you depart.
if the sea rested in my palm,
we'd escape to the furthest point together

but how do you do it, to hold a heart,
when my hands are always stained with pain?

a thousand years have already passed,
i've been looking at you for so long,
and you haven't spoken to me.

without you, i would die, but when i close my eyes, i
always know where you are—in my heart,
or inside this tear that fell onto my hand.

i was working and thinking about you
i came home and thought about you
i was calling and i was thinking about you

"how are you?" and i was thinking of you
"where do we go?" and i was thinking of you
i smiled, lowered my eyes and thought of you

i didn't know who you were with now
i didn't know what you were doing
but i sure knew what you were thinking

the city is vast,
just like the love between us.
we didn't just hope; we actively sought each other.
then fate smiled upon us, and here we are now, hand
in hand, heart to heart,
two souls intertwined as one.

the morning light shines through the window,
and i see your face,
so beautiful, so natural,
without a trace of makeup.

your hair is tousled,
your eyes are still sleepy,
and your lips are slightly parted,
as if you're about to speak.

i smile,
and my heart fills with joy,
to see you like this,
in your most natural state.

you are the most beautiful woman i have ever seen,
and i am so grateful to have you in my life.

you are, simply are,
the love of my life.

you were truly worth the wait,
a love that transcends time.

in the dance of our existence, you and i,
a cosmic intertwining beneath the sky.
threads of fate weaving silently,
our souls entangled,
beautifully.

through time's vast and endless stream,
a shared journey, like a waking dream.
no need for words, the silence speaks,
our connection strong, no end it seeks.

i never claimed to be flawless, you see,
i'll help you uncover every flaw in me.
if you find more, that's just fine,
as long as we stay intertwined.

love, love, it's a dance so sweet,
up and down the stomach, a rhythm complete.
love, love, a hole in the doughnut so round,
its fleeting sweetness makes it profound.

accept me as i am, please don't inquire,
in my mind, a world to disregard, to inspire.
i want you as my discreet confidante,
accept me, and you'll be my silk enchant.

accept me, and together we'll explore,
no need to ponder what's right, what's in store.
to the north pole or the south, take your pick,
accept me, tell me you can, be my magic trick.

endless,
to me, you are the moon and stars,
the sun and sky,
everything i desire,
all i wish to have,
endless

what lies within?
a love has bloomed, my heart did win.
now, i care not for worldly things,
for all others, their voices are but fleeting winds,
none compare to the melody of you.

how i adore you,
an emotion i can't quite define.
in the depth of my being, you align.
if you gaze into my eyes, just a glance,
you might grasp this love's sweet dance.

nothing compared to you, and yet it still does

pulse
of
*v*itality

Some may have tasted life's vast array,
 its peaks and valleys, its night and day.
My world, though, is where you stay,
I'll hold on tight, come what may,
And never wander far away.

While others love a thousand scenes,
And wander far to chase their dreams.
I, loving only you, remain serene,
In this quiet, I'll weave our joyous theme.

now and forever,
i will be with you and for you.
whatever happens,
 wherever you are,
 because there's no other place or reason to keep me
away from you
 when our hearts long to love each other

i love hearing your steps behind the door,
the jingle of keys, and the reassuring click that
intoxicates my heart.
i can smell your skin after a tiring day.
you've finally returned home.
it's just you and me inside this fabulous castle of
happiness, leaving the whole world outside.

you are my home, you are my all

in life, the possible often seems impossible,
yet our love defied the odds,
turning the impossible into our reality.

i'll be forever grateful.
you will forever be my

daily delight of love

thank you for embarking on this voyage of love.
regardless of how you choose to utilize this book,
i trust it has served as a powerful testament to the
fervor and tenderness in your life.
may your life be filled with
enduring happiness, warmth, and love.

Made in the USA
Monee, IL
08 February 2024

53140660R00111